Wednesday River

New Poetry

Barbara Hazard

Cover: *Blustery Day,* painting
Book illustrations by Barbara Hazard
www.BarbaraHazard.com

Back cover: Photography by Lloyd Wolf

Book Design by Helene Sobol
www. HeleneSobol.com

I am grateful to Donna Davis and John Fox for keeping me in touch with that poetic muse within. It's all too easy to get distracted by my more visual art, and by the everyday demands of life. I dedicate this book to both of them.

Contents

Clarinet

Beginnings

Wednesday River

The Angel of Distance

The Knitter

Casting Off

Clarinet

Three a.m.

Three a.m. I have come to the sofa
in the living room by the front window
where the moon of the street light
casts its predictable shadows.
The liquidamber, now red and gold,
trembles over the quiet street below.
No one walks, no one drives by.
No one will call.

Far away a siren.
A train calls its passing,
a plane hums over the bay.
A whiff of skunk,
of pears ripening in the kitchen,
a swelling of the earth from a day's rain.
The floor creaks.
The house breathes.

I curl into the quilt, turn on the light
and open my book.
These are sacred times.
The blessing of quiet, of diving undisturbed
into faraway lives, lives of snow, danger,
courage, betrayal—a time to dream awake,
to feed the dreams to come,
to let sleep again, softly,
draw me into its net.

The most logical place to begin

is not always the best.
Often the beginning is buried
in the midst of a terrible tangle;
by pulling on the salient thread
you will only tighten the knots.
Start softly.
Sift apart the strands.
Don't be afraid to cut.
Make some knots of your own—
the knit will hold.
Gray goes well with gold.
Slubs of overlapping color
add to texture
and if you have pieces
left over, well...
let the cat play with them,
stuff a pillow,
or save them for a rainy day.

Clarinet

I sat in the car in front of the house
while the clarinet washed over me
with its velvet sound, rooting me,
sinking me.
The edges of trees
softened and the garage doors
and the steps to the porch
and the mailbox with all its demands,

vanished.
What swam in
was the husky scent of lilac
riding on a rhythm of sun
and song, as blue
spent blossoms,
scattered on the ivy
and lifted with the wind.

I stayed
until the maple
pulled into focus,
its pale tips
pulsing with ambition,
and the clarinet
yielded to the drums
and came charging
down
the runway of the day.

Breaking Silence—

So I say to my beloved daughter
something like—I don't feel
      so sure we're going to make it.
What had we been talking about before,
sitting at the table over pea soup and toast?
And then it all falls out of my mouth
although with some other part
      of my brain
I am thinking that I am not being a good mother—
it all falls out and lies there between us—
bird flu, global epidemics, this outrageous war
that sets us up as rightful targets
      for generations to come,
my sadness for America
not only off the tracks but careening wildly
down some solitary trail—well, it all comes out:
global warming, ice caps, bees,
the Kalahari, child soldiers, child prostitutes...
the faces of my granddaughters
(to whom I would never say such things) rise up
and, my daughter and I, both in tears,
look straight at each other
and she nods.

Silence

Silence knows
the waking sounds of morning,
the shuffle to the bathroom,
the click-click on the gas stove,
the opening and shutting
of doors and windows.

Silence knows, too,
the irritation of crows
carping from the hedge,
the smother of motors
revving up by the street,
and the stealthy hum of electronics
through the air.

Silence has some secret pockets
it shares reluctantly.
You may seek earnestly,
travel far or travel deep, or
you may simply be surprised
some day at home,
after you have forgotten to look,
when you hear the voice of silence.
You will recognize it.
You have heard it before.
It may be your own true voice.

Trumpet Vine

I have been sitting on the bench
in the October sun, savoring the last
of the jasmine.
Lists of things undone, misplaced,
hover over the roof,
await me in the kitchen,
but at the moment I am seized
by two red blossoms
stretching out from the thicket
of vines on the roof—
two only,
deep velvety orange-red.
They dredge up a time of first aloneness,
a time of drawing every day,
of the sweet touch of charcoal,
full sweep of arm and line,
new powers,
new grace.

Jazz in a Time of Need

October 2002

I am listening to jazz a lot.
The Senate hearings drone on
and the ducks fall into line.
Terry Gross interviews someone
who writes about smallpox—
the airwaves pulse with death,
yet America believes in
the righteousness of war.
I am scared.

Can we stop for a minute,
savor the clear blue October sky,
listen to the sparrows, innocent of strategy,
calling in the fragrant bush?
The children sit down to supper.
We have supper here in America.
To what do they sit down in Baghdad?

Have the voices on the radio
stopped to listen to anything
besides themselves? Try a little
music, you guys, take a step or two
by yourself, in the dark. Try it!
Maybe the rhythm will catch you—
maybe you will remember nights in June
and love and easy kisses.
Then, touch someone's hand.

Election Eve, November 2008

—and what is useful to do?
Should we dig in the earth
plant vetch and potatoes,
        sow beans
and reap swallows and plums?
Could we dig for beauty
through the mud of early fall,
speak truth with grace,
earn trust, wear old clothes,
stop up the cracks in the kitchen
        windows?
How elegant the patches of this life,
the hope for hope, the singing
        in the basement,
the dreams of a sensible man
        of justice.

No Baggage, No Address

May, St Petersburg

I have landed lightly on this northern branch
and will leave again soon.
Things here are lovely, moist and full.
A peony drops blood-red petals,
rain softens the horizon with the smell
of lilacs. trains and busses
stitch the long, long day together.
The edge of the world
is no longer clear.

When I leave, invisible threads
trail in the air, ravel, unravel,
snap in the wind,
snag on bushes low to the ground
and on the lines to your house.
It is not so bad to be held,
from time to time,
fast to the ground.

Insomnia

In the silence of the night
when sleep teases
from some other realm
and the legs twitch
and thoughts run up and down
the familiar escalators of the soul,
is there something to be found?

Is there not some place,
some deep blue
pool of the heart,
where stillness waits
pulled up upon the beach,
ready to cast off?

These pale November nights
with ghost fog brushing the hedge,
and the yellow breath
of the quarter moon,
how I long
for the sound of rain.

The Rhythms of Life

The rhythms of life are everywhere—
in the dark as I wake at seven,
in the slow surge of the sea at noon,
in the pulse of my throat
as I wait for your call.

We all dance to your rhythms—
some in cadenced measured beats,
some in spurts of Charleston,
two-step, tango, whatever the beat—
but you somewhere
are calling the tune,
and when the dance is over,
the dance is over.

Epiphany

Is this God I feel
or just the body's joy
when the cat lies on my chest as I read
and his purring mirrors my heart?
Is it the body's joy
or the heart's
when you wrestle me to the ground
with your laughter and wild hair?
Is it the heart's joy
or the soul's deep knowing
when the music soars and tears come
and the body thrills to some harmony
equal to the ringing of the stars?

Appassionata

After the rising dissonance

with the trumpet and the sax
trying to out-shout each other
and the drums, the drums,
trying to shut them both down,

came the silence—two, three, five—
one hardly dared to count—
eight, thirteen...

and the cello began
in such pure and hesitant
sweetness
that the tears began to rise
and flowers of tenderness
opened slowly
and we saw each other again
in all our various and awkward beauty.

Beginnings

Beginnings

These days I am being drawn
back to the beginnings of myself,
to the room with the small blue bed
to the footsteps in the hall
to the sounds of my mother and father
        talking in the next room,
to the owl in the tree at night
        who disappeared with the dawn,
to the secrets shared in the dark
        with my elephant Elmer.

I am drawn back to the silent rebellion
        over spinach and peas—
my one small area of control—
back to the tongue-tied pupil,
the too-accommodating friend,
the closet Lone Ranger,
Sheena of the Jungle.

Am I still that person? Was she me?
Was she the root of these flowers and twigs,
the snarls and leaves of this prickly plant.
What turns under the sun,
what probes into the earth
remain? This year's buds are taut.
Something will burst out.

A Child of the Coast

I learned early the push
and seep of daily tides,
the life beneath the mud,
bubbles popping in the slick.
I knew the sweet sap that ran
under the smooth skin
of the maple and knew,
in the shag of the black oak,
what colonies explored
its vast and barky canyons.

I knew too that there was more—
more to this earth than we could see,
more to me than I could know;
knew that someday I would sing,
knew that deep inside
a golden painting waits, etched
with conundrums of the spirit,
with algebraic secrets of the stars
in the blues of all the seas
with the soft and fragile edges
of a rose.

Rainy Days

I could never be happy in the desert.
I need the sound of rain,
the thrum on the roof,
the sheeting on the window panes.
Roses lift up their heads
and drink.
Roots of the birch shiver
as the slow balm of rain
traces the script of their secret paths.

I grew up in rain, in soft
Atlantic fogs and muggy summers
with fireflies at dusk.
Earthworms coated the concrete
by the back porch as the sun
emerged, hazy, uncertain,
and the oaks dripped onto the grass,
and the maples steamed;
we wondered if it would
be dry enough for our mothers
to let us go to the beach on the 10 o'clock bus
or whether it would be another day
of paper dolls and stories
on the blue sofa
by the window.

Where I'm From

I'm from the silver spoon and the row of beans,
from my grandma's Packard with the gray fur rug
and dull round scissors for the paper dolls.
I'm from leaf piles and squirrels
from twig villages with my cousin, Sally,
The Bobbsey Twins and Heidi,
Mary Noble, Backstage Wife,
Vicks Vaporub, ice cream with flecks of black
   vanilla.
I'm from penny postcards and the ice man,
the crunch of gravel, the smell of tar,
a tumble in the gritty ocean, a noseful
of salt water, a bandaged knee,
and a rope swing strung by my father
from one of the unclimbable oaks.

Artichoke

I grow in dry soil,
in tall grasses under hot sun
and morning fog.
I ripen slowly
taking in moisture from the air
and from periodic storms.
I keep the heart of me
safe with thorns
until it is ready to open.
I confess to some stabbings,
but
leaf by leaf
I unfurl,
beginning to open
the soft throat of me
to what I know
is hard, is beautiful
and frightening
and mine.

Spring

I may have cheated on spring,
moving to California
where spring begins in December
before leaves fall from the red sycamore,
where jonquils rustle up their crisp faces
while the last golden apples
plop into the black wet earth.

How magical that eastern spring—
the first patch of brown earth
warmed by snowdrops,
forsythia, pussy willows—
the magic of waking one morning to green,
and the plaint of a mourning dove.
The woods turned from gray to rust,
from rust to pink to green.
Skunk cabbage opened in the mucky bog
and you brought your mother lilies of the valley
in a small cold fist.

Life defined its seasons sharply then—
Youth, motherhood, old age, death—
and the turning to the sun again
        and again and again.

Beech Grove

Down the clearing
past my father's just-felled oak
my sunburnt legs took me
to the hidden space
between the beech trees.
Gray smooth rocks, gray soft wrinkled
skin of the young trees.
The sun filtered copper through the August
leaves, dappled last year's fallen harvest.
It was enough to sit thinking no thoughts,
wishing no wish, listening to the rhythm
of my father's saw, to the northern buzz
of my grandmother's complaints to my mother
high up on the hill by the green porch,
to the anguished calls of my little brother,
looking for me and afraid of snakes.
I will always come back, I told myself.
Time and space deemed otherwise,
and yet...

Winter

This evening the sun blazed down
in a flare of orange and rose
and quickly gave over
to the early tide of night.
We had changed the light bulbs overhead
so the room shone with gold
and the furnace purred in the basement.

My father loved winter, loved snow,
loved the etched lines of branches stripped
of summer, rattling in the night gusts.
He loved outwitting the cold with scarves
and layers of wool, and he hummed tunelessly
as he raked the last brown leaves
from the drive.

My mother, a creature of summer,
stayed indoors. And why not?
These are days for cooking
and nights for knitting, nights
for a sniff of bourbon by a slow fire,
for thick soup and crusty bread,
a hot bath and a long book.
Perhaps a cow and some sheep
should be snuffling in the basement
while the cat plays with a ball of yarn
and the dog warms the bed.

Mother

Mom, I cannot find your picture.
Dad's I have, Grandma and Grandpa,
Gammy and Cappy, but you—
you have disappeared.
Perhaps it's not so bad,
for the slide show of my mind
has many snapshots, more lively
than a sepia photo.

I picture you, for instance, steadying me
down from the roof peak
on an autumn day; you climbing
the maple to help me find my footing;
you carrying the five-foot snake up the hill;
you trying to convince me that butter pecan
was better than vanilla, laughing
as we licked the melting cones
on the hot August streets.
How the smell of Vicks returns me
to your cool hands in the blue childhood bed,
and how knowingly you catered to my malingering
with Campbell's Soup and the AM radio.

You never liked being photographed anyway—
now the consequences are clear—we have to
remember you as we knew you,
warm and cool, shy and daring...

Blue

The drawer where I keep my scarves
still smells of you—a forlorn fragrance
of cologne and face powder
held for thirty years by faded silk.
My life has little need of silken scarves
but they usher in dry whispers
of cashmere, tweed, and of the sun
falling slant on the dusty blue
of your room.

...for my Great-Aunt, Margaret Linton

Almost every time
I use those frivolous fluted spoons you gave me,
I smile at the thought of you, wild and sturdy,
perhaps just finished hooking up your shower
out of links of hose,
alone in your basement apartment,
dipping delicately with scalloped spoon into a
brick of ice cream.

Tell me stories again—I am still wide-eyed.
Tell how you dug up skeletons in Madagascar,
tell about the spiders, the fevers, the writing,
the betrayals.
Tell how you flag down the city trolley
at the bottom of your garden.
Let me stay again in your trailer guest house
where I spent some rowdy nights
under mildewed blankets
with a damp and eager boy.

Tell me again how you love your life
and how you fight for
justice still, and let's write stories together
about jungles unexplored, seas uncrossed,
mountains never climbed, and about all the stars
who wonder how we met,
who envy us our tea, our silver spoons,
our sheer delight in mischief.

Gerda

After it came clear
that the Snow Queen
had stolen him away
she had to think

whether to go after him
or not. He had long been cooling off,
and she sensed the slivers of ice
beneath his nails

and beginning to form
around his mouth.
Sometimes when he spoke
she could almost see crystals of snow

adrift in the air between them.
And if I find him, she thought,
with the arrow of ice in his heart
and words of ice on his tongue,

have I heat enough
and heart enough
to warm him through?
I think I'll make another cup of tea.

Dancing at the Edge

She always danced
at the edge of possibility
but—sometimes
she lost her balance, or
perhaps,

was simply
carried over the edge by
the beat of the music.
Sometimes the landing
was bruising, but—

so far, not fatal.
You never really know
just where lies the edge.
You may have crossed it the minute
you began to move to the music

and the choreographer within
may have already charted the steps.
But listen! the music could change
with the whim of a clarinet,
and then...?

Wednesday River

Six Ways of Looking at a Pike

You could hear it, first thing
in the gray morning,
slap the still water
as it re-entered the river.

You could see it
lurking beneath the dock
at noon,
half asleep.

You could hear it thrash
on the line of the fisherman
who comes in his red boat
near sunset.

You could find it, torn and white.
floating in the weeds that wash up
against the shore.

You could pull apart the flesh
until only the skeleton was left,
elegant, articulate, worthy of Corot
or Picasso, with its sharp-toothed
undershot jaw still savagely grinning.

You could wonder all your life
about those dreams that dive
back under the waves as you,
in your morning fog,
try to grab them by the tail,
and you can thank the ones,
surly or not,
that allow you to catch them
in your worn and porous net.

Wednesday River

When the river woke on Wednesday
it had covered all its complications
with a sheet of silence
as impervious to the troubles
of the night before

as glass.
And yet she knew
that the river had simply
stashed away its secrets—
the slow invasive growths

that starve the fish,
the teeth of granite
scattered here and there,
the hungry flow
that eats away its banks.

Is it good to know all this?
she wondered, even as she
drank in the beauty of the still,
gray dawn, and gave thanks
for these moments offered free
        by some generous god.

Father, I Have Forgotten

Forgotten
are the Kings of England,
the dates of battles
and the farewell speech
of Julius Caesar...
        or was it Mark Antony?
Gone to some internal limbo
are sine and cosine, the square
of the hypotenuse
and how to tell the red pine
from the black.

But I remember days with you—
days in the gray beech forests of my childhood.
I remember the slow swish of oars at evening
and how the sun dropped red beyond the reeds
and the yellow moon entered the glowing sky.
Then the windows across the way
blinked orange as the earth grew dark
and we listened to the loon complain
on the slow river. Later, on the radio,
the clarinet sang of loss
and of the tenderness of time.

Granite

We are digging on the island
trying to go deep enough
to plant the basil
but everywhere is rock.

The spade scrapes granite,
slices off sod.
The skin is very thin, yet
every year lilies come up

and pokeweed and yarrow,
and the sumac have fingered down
to dark damp passages
in a world below the bone,

rich in compost,
deep in grief.

Stiff Wind

This evening—a stiff wind.
No whitecaps yet, but
a pale moon in a pale sky
rocks across the river
in the late sun.

A cup of warm tea,
a square of chocolate.
Zipped to the neck,
I listen to the far roar of engines,
the slush and gurgle of water
on the island shore, the clink
of the flag line slapping the iron pole.
Three heron flap slowly upwind to home.
The swallows that nest
above the porch light
are foraging elsewhere

It is a night for listening—
to the red freighter
pushing deep water down to Montreal,
to the speed boats thundering
upriver to the Bay,
to the starts and stops of smaller craft
in and out of these stone islands.

But now the swallows are back.
Wheeling and crying,
they chase me from my table.
The wind is chilling
and my fingers icy
around the cooling tea.
The house is calling me
with its silent voice.

When the Wind Picked Up

leaves from the birch
began to fall
spiraling from sky to porch,
dappling the punky wood
and then the steps
and then the path to your house
with tawny hearts.
In the course of a day,
a day of whitecaps
and dark bluster,
the birch stood nearly bare—
its fine filigree sectioned the sky
and the text of autumn
hummed in its branches.

End of Canadian Summer

The flag hangs still in the evening light.
Sumac flaunts new shards of scarlet
and the milkweed behind the house
has opened its velvet crust. Cormorants
in ragged hundreds sweep upriver
hugging low to the smooth gray water,
in practice for the long flight south.

I, too, am readying to leave,
stowing the matches, the candles,
triaging the clothes, the magazines,
paring down to the last cube of butter,
the last onion, last bottle of beer.

In the woods the creatures
watch this autumn ritual.
They will retake the cliff by the dock,
will fish again from the swimming rocks.
The coyotes will howl
from the hill behind the bay
and scavenge in the compost.
A new shift comes on duty.

We are only here on tolerance,
we who leave before the river cools,
before the trees shake off
their summer clothes
and dance to the winter storms.
We do not see the flat-ribbed weasels
skulk in the afternoon dark
or hear the night-time screams of rabbits.
We do not ourselves slink flat-ribbed
in the afternoon dark nor huddle
in the long night praying for the dawn.

The Angel of Distance

Island Grasses

The grasses this year,
perhaps because of all the rain,
perhaps because of you,
are long and curved
and yellow-green, all
bent towards the lower woods,
all quiet in the lee of the oaks.
The wind has brushed them
around the rocks,
rocks frost-heaved here and there,
like lavender islands rising randomly
from this lime-green sea,
like you, come randomly,
surprisingly, into my life.
I comb the grass as I go through,
honoring the grain of their desire,
savoring the damp chill of green
between my fingers.

Roses

The roses thought it was spring.
Anyone could have told them
it was only March, and
the cold could come again
with the whipping rain
but they held fast to hope
and, petal by petal,
unfurled themselves
to the hazy sun.

What do we know
of promises?
Some easy to keep,
some afloat on hope alone,
yet sometimes March takes pity—
the garden warms
and we inhale the scent
of beauty.

The Work of the Poet

The work of the poet is to
name what is holy.
Diane Ackerman

If this is our job, then
where to begin? with the clear
drop of rain that runs down your cheek?
with the curve of a lip beginning to smile?
with the smell of honeysuckle
or the voluptuous unfolding
of cow parsley in the spring?

Would it be enough to catalog
this geometry, this mathematical
precision, its ephemeral order?
Should we sound the depths of earth
and sea, carry fire in our hands,
seek what is holy in the deserts of the East?

I would rather just begin with you,
coming in out of the rain
in your wide hat. From there the whole
world opens, clear, impenetrable,
giving and taking, once and only once
ours.

Response to W.B. Yeats

Bodily decrepitude is wisdom;
young we loved each other
and were ignorant.

From *"After Long Silence"*

We would not, I think,
have loved each other young—
I had a thing for mesomorphs
and you, I see in snapshots,
were not a hunk. But now,
your craggy face and thoughtful eyes,
your questions and your snaggled smile,
stir my soul.

And what, sixty years ago and counting,
would you have seen in me?
A flighty pretty girl, slow to speak,
eager to dance, wanting to be held.
I had not the gravity then
that binds you now to me,
the gravity that binds me now
to you.

After Solstice Ritual

We walked out last night
into the December dark
having gone three times
into the nights of each other's souls.
Past, present, and future darknesses
barely illumined, unsoothed
by candlelight or dreams.

The moon, cold and full,
lit the street.
Silky fennel churned in the dark wind
and the ashes flew from our cup
into the sodden earth.
The light will come now,
not all at once, as the moon

swings on its earth-fast string,
but slowly, incrementally—a word,
a dream, a glimpse of understanding,
belief in the power of touch,
trust in the lengthening of days—
and the dark will come again
and then the light.

The Angel of Distance

The angel of distance
sits on my left shoulder
as the moon rises
over the pear tree.
Wait, she says, know the truth.
You do not have to pretend.
See this garden as it is, ripe
and deeply tilled.
These trees were planted by others
years before. Patiently nurtured,
they multiply and bloom
under the soft night sky.
I am not looking for surprises.
I am not surprised;
one can live well
on the fruit of these trees.

A Little Bit

I only want a little bit,
not your whole heart.
Give me half a heart
or a third, tell me
you're too busy to talk,
that you are in the middle
of a great project,
that you have to fly to Peru,
that your hands are covered with clay
and you can't come to the phone
until June.
I didn't want so much
when I came to you
and I cannot give so much
now you are near.
Let's try to keep the portions small.

Solitude

He was sure she watched
until the train was out of sight
but, in fact, she was racing to the car
so intent on solitude she had already
forgotten him and his devotion
and how easy it would be to wound him,
should he glance out of the window.

But how the day sparkled
now that the fog had burned away.
A flock of pelicans took off
over the marsh.
The lights were green
all down the boulevard
and Ella was singing,
singing with all her heart,
"Fly Me to the Moon."

La Journée

I took the yellows and the reds
and the ones with flowers,
a needle and thread
and went up into the hills.
My cabin was there. I needed nothing else
but music—a bit of Bach and a brace of Brubeck.
I worked all day, cut and patched,
stitched things together.
The sun came in the windows at sunset
and I lit a fire.
I'll spend the night, I thought,
maybe tomorrow I'll go down the hill
and then again, maybe not.
I might stay for a month.
I might stay for a year.
If I want to give a party
I'll call some friends
but nobody gets to spend the night.
Nobody gets to ask what I am doing tomorrow
or when I'm coming back
or what are my plans for Christmas.

Home

A home I never lived in
appears in my dreams.
I am moving in.
I have waited a long time
for the previous owners to leave.
The grasses are yellow.
Crickets silence and jump
as I climb the hill.
Years of eucalyptus shards crunch
underfoot. No one has planted
or tended, but a splayed apple tree
holds near the road.

I have never lived in such silence.
Stars wheel over an always yellow July
and frogs begin the song they learned
in another world than this.
I have drunk wine with poets
and adventurers, trekked through
birch and pine in alien valleys
and planted tulips in yards
of houses I will never see again.

Now I will live here alone,
drink tea in the sun by the window,
light the stove at night,
read and listen, knit and dream.

Healing

It's not just in the roots
that healing lies
but in the dark soil
of the forest within,
in the burnt fields
and the gray skies.

How much joy of this world
enters into us—it cleans us,
soothes and sharpens us.
It floats between the cells
of our awareness
and leaves us

light as dandelion,
solid as oak.

The Knitter

Erato

The muse
does not visit my study.
She does not like
clutter. She does not like
to-do lists or the telephone
or NPR.
It's not that she's a fanatic
for order,
it's just—she wants all
of my attention.
She does allow me to knit.
She likes me to listen
to music and sew
or to sit in the yard peeling apples,
noticing
the clouds, moved by
sad songs
of transient swallows.
Then she may come sit
beside me, may hand me
an apple, hold the yarn
or pluck me a forget-me-not
or two.

The Other

I like it when that Other one takes over,
wrests the pen from my hand,
scribbles down words long forgotten,
plays the fool, opens the windows,
steeps the tea for long long life
and plunges deep into reds
and feathers and bruises.

I think we climbed together
in the backyard maple,
learned to swim, rode the bus,
watched the owl from the small blue bed.
Sometimes now we soak in the tub
late at night,
when eastbound trains
call from the valley below
and raccoons prowl
under the steps. Then the colors
flash and twist, knot and tangle,
and thoughts, almost incomprehensible
boil up from some sweet reservoir of Other,
accessible only by grace.

Quilt

When you've taken it apart,
stitch by stitch,
for the second time
and you still don't know
what you're doing wrong—
improvement is not the only option.

What you had in mind
in the beginning seems
a bit tawdry, trite, one might say,
and chances of pulling it together
seem slight.
But you pick up a bit of red

that had fallen behind the table
and somehow the other pieces
begin to find their place.
You start to get excited again.
Improvement is now
the only option.

The Color of Rust

I am deep into the color of rust,
of the canyon earth, a river
of silt, fire of juniper
and dreams from a terra cotta
land.

A bowl of soup, a touch...
Somewhere between the worlds
of dream and day, lies the magic.
It is hoping to get a word in edgewise,
hoping for the slope of a pen,
for the rhythm of pattern and line,
rust and gray,
branch and flow.

By day I stitch birds
onto the limbs of trees. At night
I have errands in far-off lands.
I try to explain myself.
I try to listen to what the magic says,
but the crows in the apple tree
pull me back to home.

Labyrinth

Silence.
How to start
without a clue to where
to go, down into the labyrinth
with no ball of yarn
and the roaring of the minotaur
coming closer with every step. Yet
to go on, not knowing, unprepared,
without defense, to hope
to seize the horns and ride
for one short wild
and passionate fling.

If I Find the Door

—if in the dark I feel
the splintered wood
the weathered pine
with its old hinges, the latch
bent a bit and the pin
still hanging from
a worn white string....

If the grass has not grown so thick
as to block the entrance—
if it opens just enough to let me in,
then I will enter that cold musty world
of basements and stairs,
of trunks with labels from the Riviera,
from Aix and Baden Baden,
Samara and Bombay,
trunks full of tulle and pressed gardenias,
white leather gloves and sequins.

It opens a world of night and stars, of wind
roaring down the river, a world of fire
and rock and the smell of love.
Then might I comprehend
the calligraphic nonsense
from those raucous dreams
that hang the trees with pearls and fill
the sweet damp day with poems.

Pentimento

...a high flown word
meaning that you didn't like
what was on the canvas at first
and you covered it up
with another layer of paint.

You are not through with it, though.
Time has its way, and its truth...
One day you will be staring blankly
at the wall where you hung the finished piece
and you begin to see those mud-colored
streaks, the blood, and the black barbs
you thought you had hidden. It is not
your imagination—science
can confirm this. Now you will have to
peel and scrape, sponge and scrub,
until what you thought was hidden
is there for all to see.

You take a look.
Maybe by now mud and black
have become your favorite colors.
You may even be embarrassed
by the gold and peachy scrapings
on the floor, the sunrise blues
in which you thought to hide.
Maybe you see some order
in this dark chaos,
some beauty in its ferocity.
Maybe it belongs to you at last.

Pentimento—an underlying image in a painting, as an earlier painting, part of a painting, or original draft, that shows through, usually when the top layer of paint has become transparent with age.
(from Italian, pentire, to repent; from Latin paenitere)

The Yellow Painting

For thirty years now
the yellow painting inside has eluded me,
has shifted to green or tan,
or scared me with its brightness,
diverted me to safer palettes.
It teases me when I wake—
flirts, dances off to some dark corner.
But it is mine, anyway, though
it stays just out of reach,
vibrant, pulsing, smelling
a little like jasmine,
sounding a bit like Brubeck,
splashing like sparrows in a fountain
at three in the afternoon
on a hot summer day
when I've done all I could do
and it's time to go home.

Simplify, Simplify

I'd like to strip my life bare,
scrape off the dross,
live in two rooms
with a stove, ten CDs,
and a lot of yarn to play with.

I'd like to dump my paints into the trash
and draw with a stick dipped in ink.
I'm ready to burn my journals
and dance around the fire with leaves
in my hair and a yodel in my heart.

Why not give away
these relics of the past,
live out of two drawers
and let dreams
gather in the cupboards?

Then, maybe, that
yellow painting,
free and wild,
will have room
to grow into its own.

Scarf

Each day a stitch in the scarf of time,
a scarf of uncertain length, uneven texture,
multiple colors. I wear it, unfinished as it is,
strands dangling, dragging in the mud,
needles clicking, tripping me up.
It is longer, now, than my grandmother's,
whose scarf was made of silk and gray,
more ragged than my mother's,
patchy, more impetuous, with stitches dropped
here and there, but it keeps me busy
and warm. There's room in it for children
who are ready to learn to knit.
I wonder now, if a little blue right here
would do, or flecks of red. It's clearly time
to add new colors.

The Knitter

She tugs on strands of yarn
that poke up between the floorboards.
They unsnarl from under the foundation,
snagging cobwebs, mud, an occasional
worm, and glints of gold
left long ago by pirates.

She fashions them into sweaters.
Sometimes the sleeves are too long
or the neck tight. The do not fit
any of the people she gives them to,
but they please her.
She likes to knit.

She had once kept her house
so tidy there was not a hint of anything
growing in the cracks. At night, however,
things would knock on the floor below
her bed. When she called in the plumber,
he found nothing,

but when she was in the house alone
the floors bulged and heaved
as if some giant vine were pressing
to break free. Only after she bent
to pluck at threads did she begin to knit
late into the silence of the night.

One, Two, Three,

five, eight, thirteen,
and so the series goes—
the code to the branching of pines,

to sunflower spirals,
the coil of the nautilus.
Had I a head for math

I could have fallen deep into
the mysteries of structure
under flickering florescence

and probably grown pale and fat.
As it is, I wander through
my neighbors' bushes, pen in hand,

looking for math in rosemary,
in hollyhocks, in lavender
and figs.

Fibonacci

I am in my studio by nine
struggling with seams and patches,
purples, greens, seeds and stalks.
Fibonacci looks over my shoulder
counting—one, two, three, five, eight.
I haven't got it right yet
and I am plagued all day
by nature's elegant arithmetic.
Five-eight, eight-thirteen...
and all this time the reds and yellows
push their way out of the shelves.
Try the rose, perhaps, flip it
        atop the crimson.
Too bright... try restraint, measure again.
But I am getting the hang of it.
I go every morning with a problem to solve,
come home with another step taken
and a new delicious dilemma.

What use is this to anyone?
I don't know. I have to do it.
I get crabby if someone bothers me.
I haven't looked at my mail for days,
I am re-reading *Patterns in Nature*
and staring at onions and celery,
sunflowers, milkweed, sliced carrots,
peach pits, figs. Look into the heart
of anything and it is there—
order, beauty, pattern, accident...
five, eight, thirteen
twenty-one, thirty-four...

Something Pokes Her as She Sleeps

Thanks to Naomi Nye, "Jerusalem"

Something pokes her as she sleeps.
Someone inside is still trying to pass exams
in courses never attended,
trying to catch trains already leaving the platform,
looking for bathrooms in maze-like campgrounds.

Often she is searching
for her children at the zoo.
Sometimes she is kissing the husbands
of good friends, totally without guilt.
They go into a secret room to which
she has the key.
Then she forgets about the exam,
the train, the lost children.

When she attends to what is poking her,
writes down details of the campgrounds,
the bathrooms, she is rewarded
by being prodded again the next night.
This is not necessarily a blessing—
who wants to lose her children night after night?

—but the something poking her demands attention
and promises more keys to secret rooms.

Scuttle

When the lobster escaped from the pot
and hid behind the stove,
we lived with it.
Sure, it stank for a while
but it was summer—we just opened
the windows wide. But then
chickens began hatching from
the organic eggs
and ate up everything on the bottom
shelves, and the fish we brought home
from the Tokyo Market
wormed their way out of the wax paper
and slithered all across the floor.
We began to think there might be a message.

Magnolia

When the magnolia buds crack open
elbowed by the satin petals,
the sound of splitting hulls
shivers the glass in the upstairs window.
It breaches the tempo of piano and Bach,
troubles the stew, seething on the stove,
and pushes the cat out the back door.
Only after the hulls litter the driveway
do we notice that our house
has filled with the fragrance of spring.

Casting Off

In Between

I will exist at the edge,
where your vision joins
the sunlight and the rain...
                    William Stafford

I'm hanging out here

somewhere between the sunlight

and the rain. It's that in-between space—

the one between yellow and green,

between ripe and decay,

between known and forgotten.

You and I have that space

between us, that we enter

and leave. It comprises many colors,

tastes of honey, wind,

and rain from the sea.

Only occasionally do we see

the mountains clear and crisp,

bordering the limits of our lives,

while behind us waits

the deep and swelling sea.

Anything Could Happen

—tomorrow, next week,
ten years from now;
friends already are falling, struck
by a sudden blow, or eroded
by the stray small streams
       of time.

So, should I hurry?
The speckled trout lurks
just below the surface
and the raven calls from the oak.
Do we not know this?
Aren't we already walking
       a tightrope

trying not to watch our feet,
but listening to the chuff of wind
in the bushes, warming
in the late December sun,
and planning something good
to cook for dinner.

Raptor

I think I have sighted the black bird
that hovers just over my left shoulder—
a vulture, a kestrel, a kite? He dips
into view but when I turn
he is off into the dark, a silhouette
with fingered wings.

I never cared for parrots or budgies,
but I would like for this elusive raptor
to settle on my shoulder—
maybe not for long,
just time enough for us
to get acquainted.

We could speak, perhaps,
of loss, and the mysteries of love, elucidate
the reasons for his coming and going—
no promises, no appointments,
no indelicate questions—just a bit of time
face to face.

Ghost

For My ex-Mother-in-Law

I somehow got you inside me
and still, long after you left,
I am laying out the knives,
blades in, the forks beside the napkins
(on top at windy picnics only),
the picture on each plate facing the diner.

You stand beside me slicing onions,
tipping eggs into boiling water
or squishing bread and eggs and meat together
with your plump fingers. You remind me
not to wipe my hands on the dishtowel,
to back-tack at the ends of seams,
to measure twice, cut once.

I have learned not to worry
about your opinions of my friends
and of my somewhat cavalier approach
to mess—dust under the bed,
piles of unacknowledged mail—
and hope you know that you are welcome
any time you choose to visit.

What is the Soul?

For Francie Bates

You are on my mind, you,
dying, muscle by muscle,
wrestling with outrages of the body
and indignities of the body politic.

Where is the soul
if not in the resolve to speak
one's anger with the last breath,
and one's love
from which the anger rises?

Is the soul a color?
Is it absorbent?
Does it darken with age
as experience seeps in
with its streams of yellow,
blue and orange.
Does it end a muddy
mix of all our days?

But perhaps the soul is really
that flame-like essence of us,
as clean as we came into life?
However long and hard we burn it,
could it be ready, if we reached,
to show the way?

Casting Off

For Susan Manes

How you slip so softly from the edge,
lose this, lose that, lose your train of thought.
The names of children, street addresses,
houses where you used to live, all gone.
Where do you store the towels?
How do you hold the yarn for knitting?
And who is that man who enters
without knocking and makes your dinner?
Will he come again? What was his name?

Why do they look at me like this?

Naming the Islands

For Susan

Here from the shore of Grenadier
you slip softly past Hemlock,
Halfway, Jug and Chub,
past Scow, Ojibway,
all familiar waters;
past Uncle Ad's, Snug Harbor,
Owatonna, Manzanita.
Watch for shoals and rocks.
Ragnavok, Atlantis, Snakeoil.
You, more than any of us,
knew the underwater contours in our lives,
knew habits of fish, of snakes and birds
and moles, of bats. Each spring
you stood in the wind on your dock
tossing ends of yarn
to the swallows, who,
rejoicing in the sun,
whirled and dove for your gifts.

For Fran Macy

I could have made a fine mosaic
had I only saved the pieces,
but like so much else
I didn't know I'd need them.
So we eat off chipped plates and bowls
and try to remember how it used to be
when things were whole and we were younger
and you were here or at the other end of the line
with the smile in your voice and your clear eyes.

I still see you on the street
though I know it can't be true.
You left six weeks ago
once and for all, a peck on the cheek,
and off you sailed on the unknown sea.
But I see you still.
I caught a glimpse of you at Peet's
in line for coffee, and again
when I drove my daughter to the Berkeley BART.

But I see you mostly in the snow
in the gray shapka with its flaps akimbo
and a scarf snug against the wind
of a Siberian November. I see you in a taxi
leaning into conversation with the Russian driver,
or by an onion dome in blue with stars
or over Baikal beside a leafless tree
alive with faded strips of prayer.
I see you rushing down an icy platform
to buy any food on sale,
back in the bad old days of travel through Siberia.

I could make a mosaic of our times together
in gray and white, blue and gold,
here and there a flash of red, and,
though I no longer believe that seeing is believing,
my heart still leaps when I see you on the street.

Abandoned Chair with Tomatoes

For Bo Collins (1932-2009)

1.

He thought he could last until the tomatoes ripened
but the door, which had been open for so long,
drew him out into the empty field.
The sun was parching, but he caught
a whiff of freshness from the river
and, following the scent, he left us.

We found on his chair two full ripe
tomatoes. There were scuff marks
on the floor where the garter snake had come
for a drink from the dog bowl.
Everything else was in order,
but the chair cast a shadow
on the bed.

2.

The question arises—
why did he leave the tomatoes?
Are they gifts for us who find him gone,
who remember how he tended his garden
and fought with his mother in the matter
of letting tomatoes ripen on the vine?
We remember how she with her garden knife
outwitted him for years.
So, perhaps a gift to spur remembrance,
perhaps a last joke,
perhaps a message from a passing angel
reminding us to savor things
in their time.

The Waiting Room

For Fran Peavey

You have been summoned
but they have not yet opened the door
nor even given you the time
of your appointment

and so you wait.
You cannot hurry this appointment;
you tap your fingers
in the narrow waiting room
that is now your life.

You make phone calls,
you stroke your dog,
you eat a peach
slowly,
slice by slice.
We are waiting with you
but when they finally call,
you must enter by yourself.

You are ready. Everything
you needed to do is done.
Now your life is bare
of all but the essentials:
the people you love,
the dog who loves you,
a few loud shirts,
and some summer peaches.

October 7, 2010

for Fran Peavey

After you left
I sat in the garden a while.
The sky hadn't changed color
nor had the roses bloomed.
A towhee thrashed in the bushes
and the cat opened one eye
before drifting back to sleep.

That you were gone was sure—
a seamless passing at the last
through the gates to somewhere.
I sat a bit longer—
who knows how long...

listening as car doors opened and shut,
as the mailman lurched up the street
and an itinerant sparrow sang
from the roof. Then I went in
and made a cup of black coffee,
strong, without sugar or cream.

Being Here Now

Am I here, or not?
I write birthday checks
to my granddaughters
and pay my rent.
I edit the show announcement
and on the way to the studio
I remember the feel of your arms
around me and I smile, deeply.

The sky is clouding over.
I wish I had brought a sweater.
Am I here, or not?
The sun has gone under
but the studio still holds the morning heat.
Colors dance on the new black fabric.
I play a waltz in a minor key on the boom-box.

Am I missing Fran, who left us yesterday
or am I feeling your arms
around me again? At any rate,
tears are blurring the stitches
and I am no longer dancing
but sitting here suffused by time
and the poignancy of love.

Tigrasha at Night

Our cat, Tigrasha, goes out for
the evening.
He doesn't go far, we hear him
jump down from the fence.
We catch sight of him near
the front steps, but mostly,
he is quiet in the nighttime dark.
Tigrasha is not a hunter
but he attends to the path the rats run
from our compost to the neighbors'.
—Don't take me for granted, he warns,
some day I may pounce. I could,
I'm sure.

Tigrasha looks at the stars. He counts
the phases of the moon,
attends to the unfolding of leaves,
the burgeoning nasturtiums, the irises.
He dozes. He hears the bathtub
empty. The lights
in the kitchen switch off.
Another twenty minutes, he thinks,
would be just right, but already
those voices from inside
are giving him the ultimatum—
come in now or wait till morning.
He goes in, but slowly,
making them stand in the chilly doorway
in their ridiculous nighties
while he enters
stiff-legged, majestic.

Recipe for a Good Night's Sleep

Take a minute in the backyard
and look for the moon.
If you don't see it,
think about where it might be
and what it might look like tonight.
Keep looking. Maybe a star will fall.
Watch for planes heading out
to Helsinki or Saigon.
Smell the jasmine.
It's best at night.
See if the cat will curl up
in your arms.
He is black as midnight
and smells like the earth.

Don't talk to anyone.
Don't listen to messages.
Don't read the mail.

After your bath
add another blanket to the bed
and curl up with a book about
things that happened
at least a century ago—

there is nothing you can do
to change them,
don't even think about it!
Let Mr. Emerson and his wife
sort out their own lives, and

when you turn out the light,
remember how beautifully
Sarah Vaughn sang to you
in the car today.

There is nothing more
you need to do tonight.

Acknowledgements

Almost all of these poems have been written in the past five years, and most of them under the sort of duress that comes over you when the leader of your poetry group says, "Now's the time to write." Without such focus, this would have been a very short book.

I have been blessed with two group leaders: John Fox, with whom I have worked since 1986, and Donna Davis, who entered my life only a year and a half ago. John, author of *"Poetic Medicine"* and *"Finding What You Never Lost,"* and director of The Institute for Poetic Medicine in Palo Alto, meets with a small group of us bi-monthly. He usually brings in a few poems on a topic that seems relevant at the time—inspiration, noticing details, silence, world events—we read and discuss them together, and then write. John is a forgiving and open soul, and is so good at making us comfortable with each other that it has been easy to open up to whatever was simmering below the surface of my life.

Donna Davis, most of whose life work has been in theater, leads The Poetry Workshop for the Berkeley Adult School. When my friend, Lois, from John Fox's group, told me she was attending a program where she got to write three poems in each session, I was both astonished and intrigued. Donna brings in "prompts for us"—we are a group of sometimes as many as 20—we write for thirty minutes or so, we each read what we wrote twice, and comment on what we liked in the poem just read. Then we go on to another prompt. Sometimes the prompt hits the mark, sometimes not, but it is always a stimulating class where people write moving and tragic and often hilarious pieces.

Attributions

Three a.m.
Inspired by James Wright's *"Milkweed"*

Silence
"The loud voice is famous to silence, which knew it would inherit the earth before anybody said so."
From *"Famous"* by Naomi Shihab Nye

Blue
Prompt: *A forlorn fragrance*

Dancing at the Edge
Prompt: *"She always danced at the edge of possibility."*

Response to W.B. Yeats,
"Bodily decrepitude is wisdom; young we loved each other and were ignorant."
From *"After Long Silence"*

Six Ways of Looking at a Pike
"Thirteen Ways to Look at a Blackbird" by Wallace Stevens

Quilt
Prompt: *Improvement is the only option*

Something Pokes Her As She Sleeps
From *"Jerusalem,"* by Naomi Shihab Nye

Abandoned Chair with Tomatoes
Suggested by a watercolor, *"Esparragal III,"* by Maxine Relton

October 7, 2010
Prompt: *Black tea, made strong, and smoothed a bit with cream*